1850s photograph of original facade of the Alamo, courtesy of the Daughters of the Republic of Texas Library at San Antonio.

THE ALAMO

Founded as Mission San Antonio de Valero on
May 1, 1718, the Alamo was the first in a chain
of missions built along the San Antonio river. As
a mission its purpose was two-fold: first, to con-
vert the Indians; and second, to hold, extend,
and civilize the frontier for the Spanish empire.
The present site of the Alamo was selected in
1724 and the cornerstone of the chapel laid on
May 8, 1744. Destroyed by a storm, a second
stone church was begun, and in 1758 the keystone and date set in. The Alamo's history as a
mission ended in 1793 when it was closed and its
farmlands distributed among the mission Indians.

Cover, detail of Robert Onderdonk's Fall of the
Alamo, courtesy of the Friends of the Governor's
Mansion, Austin, Texas.

Earliest known photograph of the Alamo, fourteen years after the battle. Courtesy of the Daughters of the Republic of Texas Library at San Antonio.

THE ALAMO

In 1801 a cavalry unit of Spanish soldiers from El Alamo de Parras, Mexico, occupied the abandoned mission. From this association probably came the name "The Alamo."

What made the Alamo famous was the Battle.

For thirteen days 188 Texan volunteers held off 4000 Mexican troops in a battle that can be counted as one of the most dramatic and violent of all time. The Texans were fighting for their rights, and by their stand committed themselves to certain death. In the eyes of the Mexican government the Texan uprising was treasonous. The Texans were Mexican citizens. The newcomers had accepted the terms of colonization — land for allegiance — and pledged themselves to the laws of Mexico. But the oath of citizenship had been taken under Mexico's Constitution of 1824. The rules had changed.

The Texas Revolution was slow in coming. Mexico had won its independence when it ousted Spain — after three hundred years of Spanish colonialism — in 1821. The fledgling Mexican government had thirteen presidents over the next fifteen years. Times were perilous, and the new nation was weakened by ambition and intrigue.

In its infancy, the Mexican government, realizing the need to occupy the empty territory of Texas, continued the colonization policy initiated by Spain in 1821 with settlers from the United States. Immigrants from the East gladly took the oath of loyalty to Mexico, and swarmed in.

But the seeds of future conflict already had been sown. In 1824 Mexico redefined its territories, making them states. Texas was the only separate territory to lose its independence and was joined to Coahuila with the capital moved from San Antonio to Saltillo. Coahuila was allowed 11 representatives in the new state legislature, Texas only 1. As inflammatory as the lack of representation in government was the transfer of the State Archives of Texas (containing deeds and land grants of all settlers, native-born and naturalized) from San Antonio to Saltillo. Armed citizens, led by Jose Antonio Saucedo, the political chief of San Antonio, gathered in protest.

In 1830 the rumbles of discontent grew louder when the Mexican government passed the Law of April 6 prohibiting further immigration from the United States, and suspending contracts in conflict with the new law. At stake were the farmlands of thousands.

Underlying the political differences between the Mexican government and the settlers from the United States, over and above specific issues like tariffs and slavery, were cultural differences of traditions, customs, language, and religion. Still, it wasn't until the fall of 1835 that uneasy Texan land owners met in convention at San Felipe de Austin to vote on the future of Texas. This was "The Consultation of the Chosen Delegates of All Texas." The fundamental question to be voted on was whether Texans would fight for outright independence from Mexico (the War Party), or in defense of the Mexican Constitution of 1824 (the Peace Party). Santa Anna had seized control of the central government and hostilities had already begun. On November 7, 1835, the Texas delegates drafted THE DECLARATION OF CAUSES.

THE DECLARATION OF CAUSES

"Whereas, General Antonio Lopez de Santa Anna, and other military chieftains, have, by force of arms overthrown the federal institutions of Mexico, and dissolved the social compact which existed between Texas and the other members of the Mexican confederacy; now the good people of Texas, availing themselves of their natural rights, Solemnly Declare:

"That they have taken up arms in defence of their rights and liberties, which were threatened by the encroachments of military despots, and in defence of the republican principles of the federal constitution of Mexico, 1824.

"That Texas is no longer morally or civilly bound by the compact of union; yet, stimulated by the generosity and sympathy common to a free people, they offer their support and assistance to such members of the Mexican confederacy as will take up arms against military despotism.

"That they hold it to be their right during the disorganization of the federal system, and the reign of despotism, to withdraw from the union, and to establish an independent government."

Since October, San Antonio had been occupied by 1200 Mexican troops under General Martin Perfecto de Cos, while an army of Texans was encamped on the outskirts of town, undecided whether to attack or not. The major reason given for the Texan indecision was the refusal of officers of one division to march in the absence of the free negro Hendrick Arnold, who had been chosen as a leader. Benjamin Rusk Milam, who had been dispatched on a scouting tour toward the Rio Grande, and Arnold returned to find the Texans preparing to withdraw. With a roar Milam called out to the men, *"Who will go with old Ben Milam into San Antonio?"* Three hundred Texans volunteered and Hendrick Arnold guided Ben Milam's men into position for the siege of Bexar.

Benjamin Rush Milam was born in Kentucky in 1788 and fought in the war of 1812. As early as 1819 he joined the Mexican forces fighting for independence from Spain. He applied for and obtained Mexican citizenship. In 1835 Milam appeared before the legislature at Monclova concerning land titles. On his return trip he was taken prisoner along with officials from San Antonio by a detachment under General Cos. Milam escaped and reached the volunteer Texans near Goliad.

Juan Nepomuceno Seguin was born in San Fernando de Bexar (San Antonio) in 1806, son of Erasmo Seguin, influential and leading citizen. A liberal, like his father, he was elected political chief of the San Antonio district at age 28. In September 1835, when General Cos marched against the Texans, Seguin recruited a force of Mexican ranchers to fight for their rights.

Martin Perfecto de Cos was a leader under Jose Morelos in the Mexican Revolution of 1811. The brother-in-law of Antonio Lopez de Santa Anna, he was sent to Texas in September 1835 with orders to expel all American settlers who had come into Texas since 1830, disarm the Texans, and arrest all Texas patriots opposed to Santa Anna's rule.

1835: THE SIEGE OF BEXAR

Just before dawn on the morning of December 5, 1835, the Texas volunteers commanded by Ben Milam and Francis J. Johnson attacked General Cos' troops in San Antonio. Cos had stationed one force of his men in the Alamo and another behind breastworks on Main Plaza. The Texans moved forward, and for three days the battle raged with a house to house assault. On the third day Milam was killed by a rifle ball. The next day the Mexicans were driven back from Military Plaza, and at daylight on the morning of the 9th the Texans observed a white flag flying from the Alamo. General Cos signed papers of capitulation which gave the Texans all public property, money, arms, and ammunition in San Antonio, and agreed to parole his army by withdrawing it south of the Rio Grande.

The siege of Bexar was a crucial event in the history of Texas. It brought Santa Anna at the head of his army to retake San Antonio and Texas, and men indecisive about their future as Mexican citizens or Texans were moved irrevocably to independence.

"From the time the Consultation (convention) was called to the time it met, the situation had drifted into a shooting war. The fear of tyranny had become a reality. Santa Anna had seized dictatorial power, had sent an advance guard of the Mexican army (under General Cos) into Texas, and had the Constitution of 1824 annulled. The self-styled Napoleon of the West was on the march in person to the distant province to stamp out all opposition, and teach the Texans a lesson."

Castaneda, The Fight for Freedom 1810-1836, Vol. VI, Our Catholic Heritage in Texas, Austin, 1950

Imaginary sketch of the Battle of the Alamo by an artist who had only written and oral accounts to draw from, shows dramatic effect of the story. From Nile's "South America and Mexico," 1837.

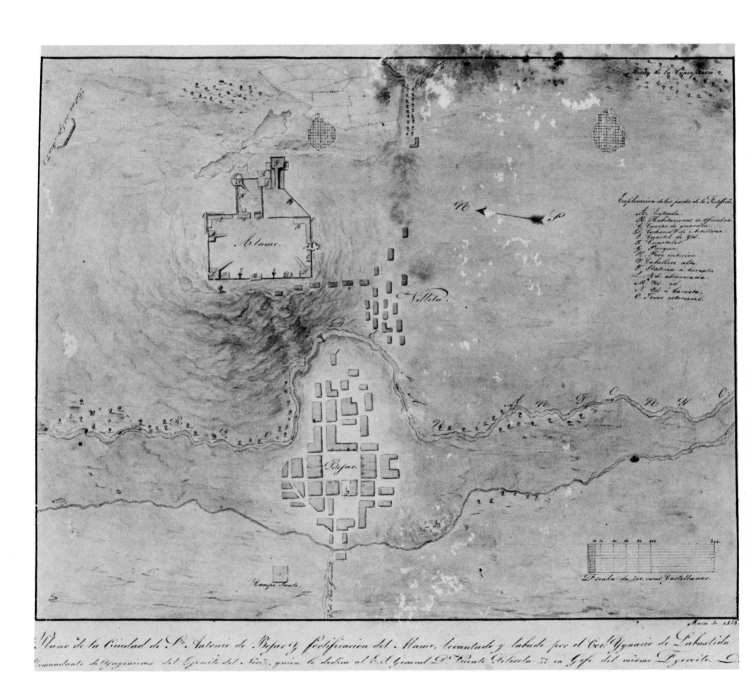

SANTA ANNA'S MAP OF THE ALAMO BATTLEFIELD and the town of San Antonio de Bexar 400 yards across the San Antonio River towards the west, with a footbridge connecting the two settlements. The outlying houses of La Villita south of the Alamo were destroyed by the defenders to deny Mexican attackers protection. At top of map, two rows of trees outline road to Gonzales. Map drawn by Col. Ygnacio de Labistida, Commander of Engineers, March 1836. Courtesy of the University of Texas Archives, map file, Austin, Texas.

Right, above: map of San Antonio de Bexar and the Alamo compiled from drawings by Captain Green B. Jameson, Texan Army, January 1836; Colonel Ygnacio de Labistada, Mexican Army, March, 1836; and Captain Reuben M. Potter, United States Army, 1841, five years after the battle.

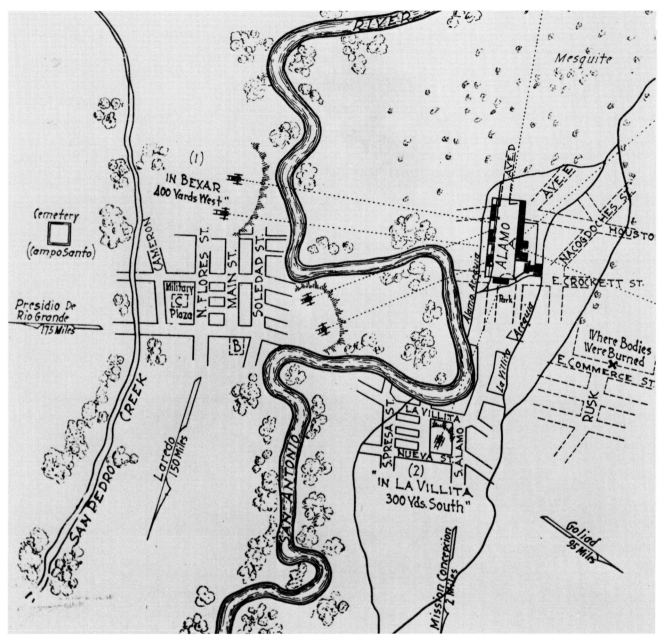

Courtesy of the Texas State Archives, Austin.

1836: THE BATTLE OF THE ALAMO

The Battle of the Alamo began on February 23 and lasted thirteen days. The final assault took place in the early morning hours of March 6, with General Antonio Lopez de Santa Anna commanding the Mexican Army from his headquarters "about five hundred yards south of the Alamo near the old bridge." Lieutenant William Barret Travis commanded the Texans from a post on the north battery. On the thirteenth day, at the sound of the bugle, three attacking columns of Mexican infantry moved in simultaneously -with one column attacking near a breach in the north wall; another the area of the chapel; and the third scaling the west barrier. The final assault lasted ninety minutes with every Texan dying at his post as room after room "was carried at the point of a bayonet."

Travis' Letter

"Commandancy of the Alamo ---
Bexar, Fbry 24th 1836 ---

To the People of Texas &
all Americans in the world ---

Fellow citizens and compatriots — I am besieged, by a thousand or more of the Mexicans under Santa Anna — I have sustained a continual bombardment & cannonade for 24 hours & have not lost a man — The enemy has demanded a surrender at discretion, otherwise, the garrison are to be put to the sword, if the fort is taken — I have answered the demand with a cannon shot, & our flag still waves proudly from the walls — *I shall never surrender or retreat.* Then, I call on you in the name of liberty, of patriotism & everything dear to the American character, to come to our aid with all dispatch —The enemy is receiving reinforcements daily & will no doubt increase to three or four thousand in four or five days. If this call is neglected, I am determined to sustain myself as long as possible & die like a soldier who never forgets what is due to his own honor & that of his country —

Victory or Death

William Barret Travis
Lt. Col. comdt."

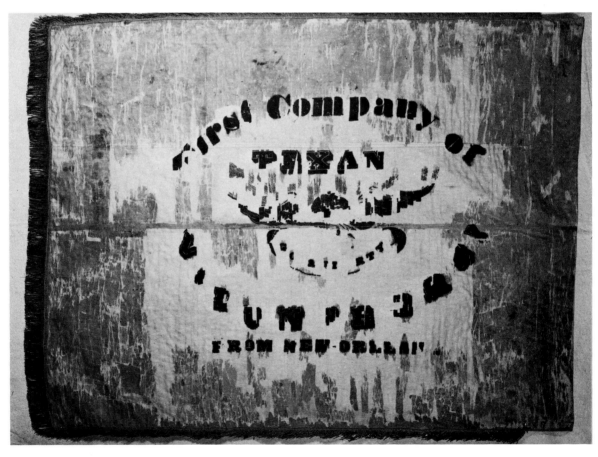

Restored remnants of the flag of the New Orleans Greys which was captured by the Mexican Lieutenant Jose Maria Torres of the Zapadores battalion. Torres tore down the Texans' flag and planted in its place the Mexican red, white and green colors emblazoned with the golden eagle. He died with his hand still on the staff. Santa Anna sent his trophy back to Mexico City where it remains today. Photograph courtesy of the San Antonio Express Publishing Company.

William Barret Travis, a Lieutenant Colonel of the Cavalry, assumed full command of the Alamo when Bowie became ill. His appeal for aid "To the people of Texas and all Americans in the world . . ." has become a part of world history. Travis was born in 1809 in the Edgefield District of South Carolina and died at the Alamo on March 6, 1836, at the age of twenty-seven. Portrait by Henry McArdle painted years after Travis death. Copy courtesy of the University of Texas Institute of Texan Cultures.

The "Deguello," or "death march," with bugle calls for the cavalry, taken from El Soldado Mejicano, signalled the dawn attack by the massed army of Santa Anna.

Antonio Lopez de Santa Anna Perez de Lebron, President of Mexico and General-in-Chief of the Army of Operations, personally directed the siege of the Alamo. Santa Anna travelled with his own striped marquee, monogrammed china, crystal decanters, and silver chamber pot. Born at Jalapa, Vera Cruz, on February 21, 1794, of Spanish parents, he died on June 22, 1876 in Mexico after living in exile. From a rare print first published in 1837 in the United States. Courtesy of the University of Texas Institute of Texan Cultures.

THE LAST DAY

Left, the Siege of the Alamo painted by Theodore Gentilz, a French artist, in 1844. Courtesy of the Daughters of the Republic of Texas Library, San Antonio. Below, the Battle, by an unknown artist, courtesy of the Texas State Library, University of Texas Institute of Texan Cultures.

On March 5, Santa Anna detailed his plan of attack for his generals: "Tomorrow morning at 4:00 the attacking columns will undertake the assault on the sounding of the bugle. General Cos will command the first column . . . Each man will carry two scaling ladders . . . the men carrying the ladders will sling their rifles on their backs until the ladders are properly placed. The men will not wear cloaks or carry blankets. The troops will wear shoes or sandals. All chin straps will be in order, and all weapons will be made ready, especially the bayonets."

The Battle raged with desperate fury, the Texans' fire so fierce that they repulsed the enemy's attacking column three times. When Santa Anna's reserves threw up the ladders, Mexican soldiers cut their way onto the parapets and swarmed through the breaches in the walls. The Texans were forced back foot by foot, room by room, fighting all the way, with Davy Crockett and his Tennessee Boys swinging their rifles like clubs. In ninety minutes every Texan had been killed. Courtesy of the Daughters of the Republic of Texas Library, San Antonio.

"Dawn at the Alamo" by Henry McArdle, completed at turn of century after years of research. Travis fought atop the north battery, inspiring the men with his shouts, "Hurrah, my boys!," encouraging the men of Seguin's company on in Spanish, until he was felled by a shot in the head. Davy Crockett is shown lower right in a hand-to-hand last stand, using his rifle-butt as a club, with his Tennesseans holding the Mexican troops at bay with a fury that marked them forever for world acclaim. A brave young Mexican Lieutenant of the Zapadores battalion, Jose Maria Torres, fought and clawed his way to the roof of the long barrack, tore down the grey and blue silk flag of the New Orleans Greys, the flag of the Texans, and planted the Mexican colors, the red, white and green emblazoned with the eagle. Torres fell with his hand still on the staff, a hero to his people. 189 Texans took on 4000 Mexican troops. The battle lasted thirteen days, with the final assault at dawn on March 6, 1836, lasting 90 minutes, and the battle cry "Remember the Alamo" echoing throughout time as a battle cry for freedom.
Courtesy of the Texas State Capitol. Copy at the University of Texas Institute of Texan Cultures.

The legend of Travis drawing a line with his sword. When he no longer expected aid, the commander asked those who were prepared to die with him to cross the line. The legend was probably based on fact as Travis could see a battle to the death and gave the men an opportunity to leave the fated garrison. Only one man is said to have made the decision to leave. Painting by Louis Eyth, 1870. Courtesy of the Daughters of the Republic of Texas Library at San Antonio.

Burial of Heroes of the Alamo

The Telegraph and Texas Register, March 28, 1837:

"In conformity with an order from the general commanding the army at headquarters, Colonel Seguin (who took command of San Antonio for the Texans after the battle of San Jacinto), with his command stationed at Bexar, paid the honors of war to the remains of the heroes of the Alamo; the ashes were found in three places, the two smallest heaps were carefully collected, placed in a coffin neatly covered with black, and having the names of Travis, Bowie and Crockett engraved on the inside of the lid, and carried to Bexar and placed in the parish church, where the Texan flag, a rifle and a sword were laid upon it for the purpose of being accompanied by the procession, which was formed at 3 o'clock on the 25th of February (1837); the honors to be paid were announced in orders of the evening previous, and by the tolling knell from daybreak to the hour of interment; at 4 o'clock the procession moved from the church in Bexar in the following order:

"Field officers, staff officers, civil authorities, clergy, military not attached to the corps and others, pallbearers, coffin, pallbearers, mourners and relatives, music, battalion, citizens.

"The procession then passed through the principal street of the city, crossed the river, passed through the principal avenue on the other side, and halted at the place where the first ashes had been gathered. The coffin was then placed upon the spot, and three volleys of musketry were discharged by one of the companies; the procession then moved to the second spot, whence part of the ashes in the coffin had been taken, where the same honors were paid; the procession then proceeded to the principal spot and place of interment, where the graves had been prepared; the coffin had been placed upon the principal heap of ashes, when Colonel Seguin delivered a short address in Spanish, followed by Major Western in English, and the ashes were buried."

In 1899, when Colonel Seguin was in his eighties, he stated that he had buried the casket with the remains outside the sanctuary railing, near the steps in the old San Fernando Church. In 1936, repair work on the altar railing of the Cathedral led to the unearthing of a box containing charred bones, rusty nails, shreds of uniforms and buttons, particles of coal, and crushed skulls. From the discovery arose a controversy which continues today. Many historians believe that the bones uncovered in 1936 are the bones of the heroes of the Alamo.

FALL OF THE ALAMO, AND MASSACRE OF TRAVIS AND HIS BRAVE ASSOCIATES

by Francis Antonio Ruiz

On the 23d day of February, 1836, (2 o'clock P.M.,) Gen. Santa Anna entered the city of San Antonio with a part of his army. This he effected without any resistance, the forces under the command of Travis, Bowie, and Crockett having on the same day, at 8 o'clock in the morning, learned that the Mexican army was on the banks of the Medina river, they concentrated in the fortress of the Alamo.

In the evening they commenced to exchange fire with guns, and from the 23d of February to the 6th of March (in which the storming was made by Santa Anna) the roar of artillery and volleys of musketry were constantly heard.

On the 6th of March, at 3 o'clock A.M.,. Gen. Santa Anna at the head of 4000 men advanced against the Alamo. The infantry, artillery, and cavalry had formed about 1000 varas (a vara measures 33 inches) from the walls of said fortress. The Mexican army charged and were twice repulsed by the deadly fire of Travis' artillery, which resembled a constant thunder. At the third charge the Toluca battalion commenced to scale the walls and suffered severely. Out of 800 men, 130 were only left alive.

When the Mexican army had succeeded in entering the walls, I, with the Political Chief, (Gefe politico,) Don Ramon Musquiz, and other members of the Corporation, accompanied the Curate, Don Refugio de la Garza, who, by Santa Anna's orders, had assembled during the night at a temporary fortification erected in Potrero street, with the object of attending the wounded, etc. As soon as the storming commenced, we crossed the bridge on Commerce street with this object in view, and about 100 yards from the same a party of Mexican dragoons fired upon us and compelled us to fall back on the river and place we occupied before. Half an hour had elapsed when Santa Anna sent one of his aid-de-camps with an order for us to come before him. He directed me to call on some of the neighbors to come up with carts to carry the dead to the Cemetery, and also to accompany him, as he was desirous to have Col. Travis, Bowie, and Crockett shown to him.

On the north battery of the fortress lay the lifeless body of Col. Travis on the gun-carriage, shot *only* in the forehead. Toward the west, and in the small fort opposite the city, we found the body of Col. Crockett. Col. Bowie was found dead in his bed, in one of the rooms of the south side.

Santa Anna, after all the Mexicans were taken out, ordered wood to be brought to burn the bodies of the Texians. He sent a company of dragoons with me to bring wood and dry branches from the neighboring forest. About 3 o'clock in the afternoon they commenced laying the wood and dry branches, upon which a file of dead bodies was placed; more wood was piled on them, and another file brought, and in this manner they were all arranged in layers. Kindling wood was distributed through the pile, and about 5 o'clock in the evening it was lighted.

The dead Mexicans of Santa Anna were taken to the graveyard, but not having sufficient room for them, I ordered some of them to be thrown in the river, which was done on the same day.

Santa Anna's loss was estimated at 1600 men. These were the flower of his army.

The gallantry of the few Texians who defended the Alamo was really wondered at by the Mexican army. Even the Generals were astonished at their vigorous resistance, and how dearly victory had been bought.

The Generals who, under Santa Anna, participated in the storming of the Alamo, were Juan Amador, Castrillon, Ramirez, Sesma, and Andrade.

The men burned numbered 182. I was an eye-witness.

Signed, FRANCISCO ANTONIO RUIZ.

P.S. - My father was Don Francisco Ruiz, a member of the Texas Convention. He signed the Declaration of Independence on the 2d of March, 1836.   F. A. R.

Translation by J.A. Quintero, Texas Almanac 1857-1873, Waco.

THE ALAMO ABANDONED

Sketch of the Alamo from "Texas," by British Consul Arthur Ikin, London 1841.

After the fall of the Alamo the ruins of the old chapel building were deserted and left to deteriorate. In 1842 the Catholic Church petitioned the young Republic of Texas for its return but could not raise the funds to restore it as a place of worship. In 1849 the United States Army rented the property, restored the chapel building, and built the rounded top on the existing facade. In 1861 the Alamo was surrendered to the Confederacy, but at the end of the Civil War it was returned to the United States Army which continued to rent it as a depot until 1876. That same year, 1876, Honore Grenet, a French-born merchant, bought the property on the north side of the Alamo and built his "Palace," a general store over the long barrack.

The Alamo - Mission San Antonio de Valero, oil painting by Theodore Gentilz, a French settler who painted the ruins in 1844. Courtesy of St. Mary's University, San Antonio.

Condition of the Alamo in 1840s. Santa Anna flew the flag of "no quarter" from the steeple of San Fernando Church in the distance. Drawn by Lt. Edward Everett of the United States Army when stationed in the Alamo, Senate Document No. 32, Thirty-first Congress.

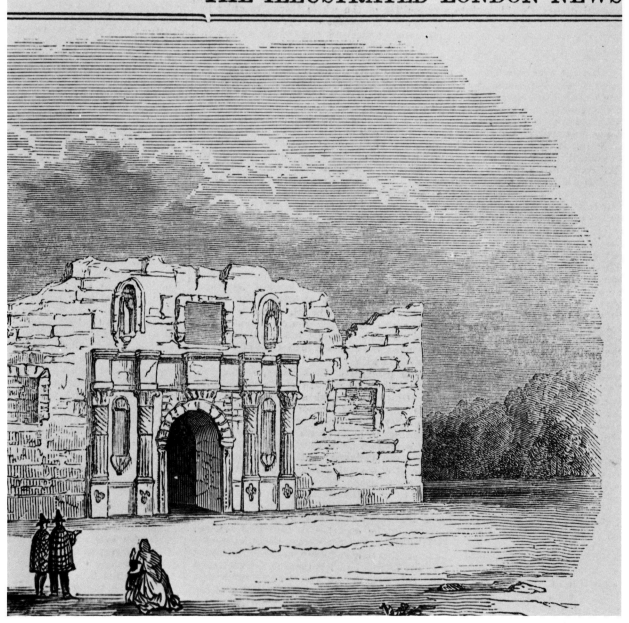

THE ILLUSTRATED LONDON NEWS

Drawing of the Alamo in ruins, by artist-reporter for the Illustrated London News, June 15, 1844.

The Historic Alamo and Grenet Business Emporium.

A BONANZA FOR SALE.

The illustration on the preceding page, and which also is the frontispiece of this book, gives an excellent view of the historic Alamo, the Thermopylæ of America, as it is to-day. When the memorable sacrifice of 1836 was complete, and bodies of the heroic martyrs had been partially reduced to ashes, the bloodthirsty Santa Anna marched his troops East to meet their richly-merited doom, leaving the Alamo a battle-scarred ruin. Fourteen years later, the Church Building, that which is now known as The Alamo, was rebuilt in its present condition on the old walls, and the Convent Building was used by the United States as a Quartermaster's Depot. On the completion of the present United States Quartermaster's Depot and Military Headquarters, a few years since, the United States Government gave up its lease of the property, and the late

HONORE GRENET,

a native of La Belle France, and a leading citizen and wealthy merchant of San Antonio, a princely benefactor of many local institutions, of unbounded liberality and great public spirit, as well as business enterprise, purchased from the Roman Catholic Church the Convent Building and yard, and altered it at great expense into its present form, converting it into an immense Wholesale and Retail Store, where he continued up to the time of his death, in the early part of 1882, to do a business in **Groceries, Provisions, Dry Goods, Queensware, Glassware, Boots, Shoes, Whiskeys, Wines, Beer, Cigars, Tobacco, and Country Produce**, second to none in this city. Besides purchasing the Convent Building and yard, Mr. Grenet leased the old Alamo itself for a term of ninety-nine years, and converted it into a Warehouse, adjoining his immense Store.

Since the decease of Mr. Grenet, his Executor, MAJOR JOSEPH E. DWYER, has successfully carried on the immense business thus left in his charge, and is now settling the estate as rapidly as possible, and as one part of his duty he now offers this mammoth Store,

For Lease or For Sale,

to the purchaser of its valuable and constantly kept-up stock of Goods, together with the lease of THE ALAMO, and the goodwill of the business, so long and so profitably enjoyed by its deservedly popular founder.

The location on Alamo Plaza, and with an extensive frontage on East Houston Street, also facing Avenues D and E, and with the Street Cars passing it every few minutes during the day, and until late at night, makes this one of the most eligible business sites in San Antonio. This property will prove to be *a Genuine Bonanza* to its purchaser or lessee. For terms and further particulars, address

MAJOR JOSEPH E. DWYER, Executor Grenet Estate,
SAN ANTONIO, TEXAS.

Newspaper advertisement from the San Antonio Light Collection. Photocopy from the University of Texas Institute of Texan Cultures, San Antonio.

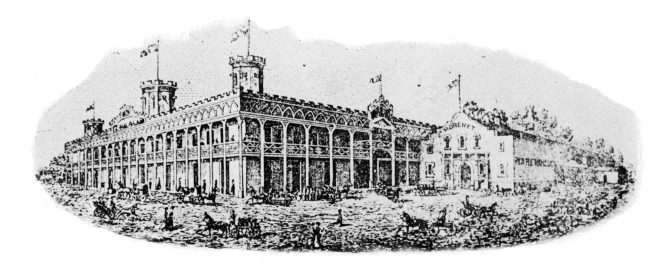

Etching of Honore Augustine Grenet store at site of the convent building of the Alamo. Courtesy of the University of Texas, Texana Collection. Copy from the University of Texas Institute of Texan Cultures.

THE PLAZA

For a hundred and twenty-five years, there was no plaza at the Alamo. Only the mission compound, enclosed by the outer walls of Mission San Antonio de Valero, rose above the open space between the mission and the river. The defenders of the Alamo could look straight across the area and clearly see the tower of San Fernando. Not until Texas joined the Union and the U.S. government took over the property did life return to the area.

From 1849 until 1859, the Alamo echoed with the thunder of army wagons. In 1854, Frederick Law Olmsted visited San Antonio. The future landscape architect of New York's Central Park described the Alamo and the area around it as "A few irregular stuccoed buildings huddled against the old church in a large court surrounded by a rude wall, the whole used as an arsenal . . . . The church-door opens on the square . . . ."

Slowly, the plaza took shape and color. First a few small houses were built, then a merchant or two ventured an enterprise, and Alamo Plaza began. In 1859 William Menger opened the doors of his hostelry on the southeast corner of the plaza, still far from the hubbub of business and government activity on Main and Military Plazas, with all three plazas linked by Commerce Street.

By the 1870's, Alamo Plaza had taken its present shape. From here the first street cars, drawn by mules, set out daily on the two mile journey to San Pedro Springs. Honore Grenet built his "Palace" on the walls of the Alamo's convent, stage lines began their journeys at the Menger's front door; carpenters and builders, a lumber yard, blacksmiths, barbers, a restaurant, boarding houses, and the iron-balconied Maverick Bank overlooked the now bustling Plaza. A City Meat Market stood out in the center, more or less where the latest bandstand is located; the first of three Post Offices, which were to lend importance to the area, occupied the elegant Gallagher Building; livery stables were located just around the corner and later provided stylish transportation to music lovers at the Grand Opera House, which opened in 1888. There were numerous bars, Julius Joske's Store, Scholz's Palm Garden, and even a Chinese Laundry. Alamo Plaza captured it all, mirroring life in the fastest growing city in the largest state, and would remain through all the years the most visited plaza of one of the world's most honored shrines.

The Alamo used as quartermaster depot by the United States Army in the 1850's. Photo from the Grandjean Collection, courtesy of the Daughters of the Republic of Texas Library, San Antonio.

View across Alamo Plaza showing Alamo Saloon at right and H. Grenet's "Palace" built alongside the Alamo church building in the 1870s and 1880s. Courtesy of the Daughters of the Republic of Texas Library, San Antonio.

View across Alamo Plaza showing the City Meat Market in the center, and H. Grenet's "Palace" built along-side the Alamo church building in the 1870s and 1880s. From the Grandjean Collection, courtesy of the Daughters of the Republic of Texas Library, San Antonio.

The Alamo dressed for the Battle of Flowers, 1896. Courtesy of the Daughters of the Republic of Texas Library, San Antonio.

Mesquite block paving was laid down in the 1900s. Courtesy of the Daughters of the Republic of Texas Library at San Antonio.

Chili queens reigned over the Plaza after dark, and it became an open-air bazaar, a gathering place for San Antonians. Looking northeast across Alamo Plaza, the United States Post Office (moved from the Gallagher Building), Hugo and Schmeltzer store, Mexican chili stands and wagon peddlers, 1900. By Jessie Thomson, courtesy of the University of Texas Institute of Texan Cultures Collection.

Looking north over the Plaza. Alamo at right. Late 1890s. Courtesy of the Daughters of the Republic of Texas Library, Postcard Collection.

San Antonians celebrating visit of President Theodore Roosevelt to the Alamo in 1905. Postcard collection. Courtesy of the Daughters of the Republic of Texas Library, San Antonio.

THE CITY'S LIVING ROOM

Diva Emma Abbott and her Opera Company celebrated the opening of the Grand Opera House, while across the plaza soft sounds of laughter and guitar sifted through. The plaza became the living room of this frontier outpost. Here it welcomed presidents, beginning with Benjamin Harrison, and here it began and ended its parades. After dark the flickering glow of kerosene lamps lighted the long tables of the chili queens, and the spice-laden aromas of Mexico and Texas were wafted about on the cool breeze coming up from the Gulf.

The Alamo overlooked it all - and still does - casting its spell, reminding men of heroism and great deeds.

With electricity and the telephone, San Antonio became the Bagdad of the brush. Photograph of the Alamo emblazoned with "incandescents" for Christmas in the early 1880s, courtesy Daughters of the Republic of Texas Library at San Antonio.

The Grand Opera House on Alamo Plaza, constructed at a cost of $150,000, opened on December 19. Notables to appear on its stage were Edwin Booth and Joseph Jefferson. Courtesy of the Daughters of the Republic of Texas Library at San Antonio.

Jan. 19th 1892

1880s parade with Grand Opera House at right, center. Courtesy San Antonio Fiesta Association.

DAUGHTERS OF THE REPUBLIC OF TEXAS

In 1883, the State of Texas purchased the ruins of the Alamo chapel from the Roman Catholic Church and placed the property in the custody of the City of San Antonio with conditions for its care. Two years later, in 1885, the State gave the church building to the city. It was not until 1905, twenty years later, that the State purchased the store over the barrack and clearing of the area began. That same year the State gave custody of the entire site, the Alamo mission-fort, the convent and long barrack, to the Daughters of the Republic of Texas, many of whom are descendants of the heroes of the Alamo. As custodians, the Daughters operate and maintain the Alamo without cost to the State.

Alamo Plaza on July 4, 1898. Courtesy of the San Antonio Conservation Society.

In 1876, Honore Grenet bought the property on the north side of the Alamo and built his "Palace," a general store over the long barrack. About thirty years later, the State purchased the store over the barrack and cleared the area. Part of the original walls of the old mission-fortress were revealed with the stripping back.

Looking due south, Alamo Plaza circa 1908, shows long barrack at left. Long barrack was covered over by Honore Grenet's wooden frame "Palace" store front in the 1870s. It was bought at auction by Hugo and Schmeltzer in 1880s. During the Mission Period, the building contained the living quarters for the priests, a dining hall, and a kitchen. The second floor served as a hospital while it was occupied by different armies. The second floor was removed in the 1900s.

The return of the 36th and 90th Divisions U.S. Army in 1919 was celebrated with a military parade down the city's main streets and climaxed with a watermelon feast on Alamo Plaza. A huge Arc de Triomphe was constructed in front of the Alamo, and long tables laden with the fruit readied. Photograph courtesy of the Daughters of the Republic of Texas Library, the Ernst Schuchard collection.

Left, Fiesta Parade, April 1931. The Alamo, the Plaza, St. Joseph's Church Spire. From the San Antonio Light Collection, Courtesy of the University of Texas Institute of Texan Cultures.

The Alamo visited by Franklin Delano Roosevelt, President of the United States, and Maury Maverick, Congressman from San Antonio during Texas Centennial year 1936. From the San Antonio Light Collection courtesy of the University of Texas Insitute of Texan Cultures.

Interiors of the Alamo Shrine between the years
of early 1900s and 1930s. The Alamo has been
under the care of the Daughters of the Republic
of Texas since 1905. They have maintained it
with a volunteer corps of history conscious wo-
men, free of charge to the public, and open seven
days a week throughout the year.

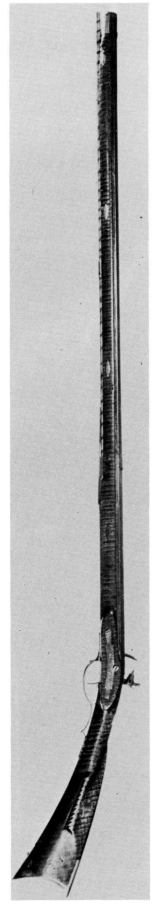

Dickert rifle used by Texans who were experts in weaponry. Mexican soldiers carried English surplus **escopetas** *which were out-of-date. Many in the attacking army were inexperienced recruits from Zacatecas and Yucatan (Santa Anna was quelling a rebellion in liberal Yucatan when General Cos surrendered at Bexar). Cannon below was used in battle. Courtesy of the Daughters of the Republic of Texas Library at San Antonio.*

HEROES OF THE ALAMO

Died In Battle March 6, 1836

Juan Abamillo, San Antonio
R. Allen
Miles DeForest Andross
Micajah Autry, North Carolina
Juan A. Badillo, San Antonio
Peter James Bailey, Kentucky
Isaac G. Baker, Arkansas
William Charles M. Baker, Missouri
John J. Ballentine
Robert W. Ballentine, Scotland
John J. Baugh, Virginia
Joseph Bayliss, Tennessee
John Blair, Tennessee
Samuel B. Blair, Tennessee
William Blazeby, England
James Butler Bonham, South Carolina
Daniel Bourne, England
James Bowie, Tennessee
Jesse B. Bowman
George Brown, England
James Brown, Pennsylvania
Robert Brown
James Buchanan, Alabama
Samuel E. Burns, Ireland
George D. Butler, Missouri
Robert Campbell, Tennessee
John Cane, Pennsylvania
William R. Carey, Virginia
Charles Henry Clark, Missouri
M. B. Clark
Daniel William Cloud, Kentucky
Robert E. Cochran, New Jersey
George Washington Cottle, Tennessee
Henry Courtman, Germany
Lemuel Crawford, South Carolina
David Crockett, Tennessee
Robert Crossman, Massachusetts
David P. Cummings, Pennsylvania
Robert Cunningham, New York
Jacob C. Darst, Kentucky
John Davis, Kentucky
Freeman H. K. Day
Jerry C. Day, Missouri
Squire Daymon, Tennessee
William Dearduff, Tennessee
Stephen Dennison, England
Charles Despallier, Louisiana
Almaron Dickinson, Tennessee
John H. Dillard, Tennessee
James R. Dimpkins, England
Lewis Duel, New York
Andrew Duvalt, Ireland
Carlos Espalier, San Antonio
Gregorio Esparza, San Antonio
Robert Evans, Ireland
Samuel B. Evans, New York
James L. Ewing, Tennessee
William Fishbaugh, Alabama
John Flanders, Massachusetts
Dolphin Ward Floyd, North Carolina
John Hubbard Forsyth, New York
Antonio Fuentes, San Antonio
Galba Fuqua, Alabama

William H. Furtleroy, Kentucky
William Garnett, Tennessee
James W. Garrand, Louisiana
James Girard Garrett, Tennessee
John E. Garvin
John E. Gaston, Kentucky
James George
John Calvin Goodrich, Tennessee
Albert Calvin Grimes, Georgia
Jose Maria Guerrero, Laredo, Texas
James C. Gwynne, England
James Hannum
John Harris, Kentucky
Andrew Jackson Harrison
William B. Harrison, Ohio
Charles M. Haskell, (Heiskell), Tennessee
Joseph M. Hawkins, Ireland
John M. Hays, Tennessee
Patrick Henry Herndon, Virginia
William D. Hersee, England
Tapley Holland, Ohio
Samuel Holloway, Pennsylvania
William D. Howell, Massachusetts
William Daniel Jackson, Ireland
Thomas Jackson, Ireland
Green B. Jameson, Kentucky
Gordon C. Jennings, Connecticut
Damacio Jimenes
Lewis Johnson, Wales
William Johnson, Pennsylvania
John Jones, New York
Johnnie Kellog
James Kenney, Virginia
Andrew Kent, Kentucky
Joseph Kerr, Louisiana
George C. Kimbell (Kimble) New York
William P. King, Texas
William Irvine Lewis, Virginia
William J. Lightfoot, Virginia
Jonathan L. Lindley, Illinois
William Linn, Massachusetts
Toribio D. Losoya, San Antonio
George Washington Main, Virginia
William T. Malone, Georgia
William Marshall, Tennessee
Albert Martin, Rhode Island
Edw. McCafferty
Jesse McCoy, Tennessee
William McDowell, Pennsylvania
James McGee, Ireland
John McGregor, Scotland
Robert McKinney, Ireland
Eliel Melton, Georgia
Thomas R. Miller, Tennessee
William Mills, Tennessee
Isaac Millsaps, Mississippi
Edward F. Mitchusson, Virginia
Edwin T. Mitchell, Georgia
Napoleon B. Mitchell
Robert B. Moore, Virginia
Willis Moore, Mississippi
Robert Musselman, Ohio
Andres Nava, San Antonio

George Neggan, South Carolina
Andrew M. Nelson, Tennessee
Edward Nelson, South Carolina
George Nelson, South Carolina
James Northcross, Virginia
James Nowlan, Ireland
George Pagan, Mississippi
Christopher Parker, Mississippi
William Parks, North Carolina
Richardson Perry, Texas
Amos Pollard, Massachusetts
John Purdy Reynolds, Pennsylvania
Thomas H. Roberts
Isaac Robinson, Scotland
James Robertson, Tennessee
James M. Rose, Virginia
Jackson J. Rusk, Ireland
Joseph Rutherford, Kentucky
Isaac Ryan, Louisiana
Mial Scurlock, North Carolina
Marcus L. Sewell, England
Manson Shield, Georgia
Cleveland Kinlock Simmons, South Carolina
Andrew H. Smith, Tennessee
Charles S. Smith, Maryland
Joshua G. Smith, North Carolina
William H. Smith
Richard Starr, England
James E. Stewart, England
Richard L. Stockton, Virginia
A. Spain Summerlin, Tennessee
William E. Summers, Tennessee
Wm. D. Sutherland, Alabama
Edward Taylor, Tennessee
George Taylor, Tennessee
James Taylor, Tennessee
William Taylor, Tennessee
B. Archer M. Thomas, Kentucky
Henry Thomas, Germany
Jesse G. Thompson, Arkansas
John W. Thomson, North Carolina
John M. Thruston, Pennsylvania
Burke Trammel, Ireland
William Barret Travis, South Carolina
George W. Tumlinson, Missouri
James Tylee, New York
Asa Walker, Tennessee
Jacob Walker, Tennessee
William B. Ward, Ireland
Henry Warnell, Arkansas
Joseph G. Washington, Tennessee
Thomas Waters, England
William Wells, Georgia
Isaac White, Kentucky
Robert White
Hiram J. Williamson, Pennsylvania
William Wills
David L. Wilson, Scotland
John Wilson, Pennsylvania
Anthony Wolfe, England
Claiborne Wright, North Carolina
Charles Zanco, Denmark
John, Negro

Pilgrimage to the Alamo, April 22, 1968, with Crockett Elementary School students clad in Davy Crockett buckskins and raccoon caps. Officially opening a week of Fiesta, students, organizations and clubs from throughout the State march quietly through the streets of San Antonio to lay flower wreaths at the Alamo in memory of the heroes who died there in 1836. Courtesy of the San Antonio Express Publishing Company.

Important Dates for the Alamo

Early Beginnings

1691   San Antonio River discovered and named by the Teran-Massanet Spanish expedition on June 13th, feast day of St. Anthony de Padua.

1709   The Espinosa-Olivares-Aguirre expedition encamped at same site, also chronicled the naming of the San Antonio. Olivares, a Franciscan missionary, noted beauty and advantages of the area.

1716   The Spanish Council of War approved the request of Father Antonio de San Buenaventura y Olivares to establish a mission on the San Antonio along with its approval for the establishment of a presidio (fort) by Captain Domingo Ramon.

1718   Martin de Alarcon, Governor of Texas, was issued orders for the establishment of permanent barracks at the Presidio of San Antonio.

Father Olivares merged his Mission San Antonio de Padua with an older mission moved from the Rio Grande and renamed the new mission San Antonio de Valero, to honor the Viceroy of Mexico, the Marquis de Valero.

The Mission Period

1718   On May 1st Mission San Antonio de Valero was officially founded on the west bank of the San Antonio River, along with the township of San Antonio.

1719   In June the mission was moved to its second site on the east bank of the river in the vicinity of St. Joseph's Church.

1722   The Presidio San Antonio was moved to its present site on Military Plaza where permanent quarters were constructed for the soldiers.

1724   Mission San Antonio de Valero was moved to its third and final location, the present Alamo Plaza.

1727   Construction of a permanent, two story structure, on the location of the Long Barrack was begun. The first floor was five equal size rooms with the stairs located in the center section. The south end contained the living quarters for the priests, the offices and a dining hall and kitchen.

1744   On May 8 the first stone church was begun. When this was destroyed by a storm, construction was begun again.

1756   The second stone church, the present Alamo, was begun but was never completed in its mission days.

1758   The keystone was dated and set in, but building was still going on.

1762   The upper part of the church collapsed and was never fully repaired.

1790   Indian population dropped from a high of some 300 to only 48.

1793   By order of the Spanish government, and in accordance with its founding rules, the Mission San Antonio de Valero was closed down, as were all the missions in the area, and its lands distributed among the remaining 39 mission Indians.

During those early years of the Mission period, the Indian Tribes living at San Antonio de Valero included members of the Lipan Apaches, Sanas, Scipxames, Tamiques, Tops, Cocos, Jaranames, Pataguas, Payayas, Yierbipiames, Yutas and Kiowas.

The Alamo

1801   A Spanish Cavalry unit stationed in Mexico was sent to occupy the old mission. This "Second Flying Company of San Carlos de Parras" came from the pueblo in Mexico - El Alamo de Parras. Although the township of San Antonio was shaded by stands of alamo trees (poplars or cottonwoods), it is believed that the name Alamo was given to the compound because of the popularity of the soldiers from el Alamo, Mexico.

1806
1814   The convento of the former mission was turned into a hospital.

1812   Church records and religious activities were moved to San Fernando Church. Until this date the chapel was in use.

1813   The Army of the North (the Gutierrez-McGee expedition) captured San Antonio and proclaimed the First Independent Republic of Texas and flew their Green Flag. That same year at the Battle of the Medina River (a major tributary of the San Antonio), the Spanish royalist force under Joaquin de Arredondo defeated the revolutionary forces and put an end to the First Republic. A young Spanish Army dragoon, Lieutenant Antonio Lopez de Santa Anna, was cited for bravery.

1819   On February 22 the Adams-Onis (or Florida) Treaty was signed, renounced U.S. claim to Texas, the boundary for western Louisiana separating Louisiana and Spanish Texas.

James Long organized the Long Expedition that provided a provisional government which declared the independence of Texas, voted on sale of land. Governor Antonio Martinez of San Antonio dispatched Colonel Ignacio Perez with 500 men to drive American settlers out of East Texas. Long escaped but returned to join forces with Mexican liberals. With fifty-two men Long captured La Bahia, near San Antonio, but four days later surrendered to Ignacio Perez.

1820   Moses Austin petitioned the Spanish Governor Martinez in San Antonio for a permit to settle Americans in Texas. The entire population of Texas was only some 4,000.

1821   Mexico ousted Spanish government and declared its independence.

Realizing the need to occupy the vast area of Texas with settlers, the Mexican government continued the colonization policy initiated by the Spaniards. Immigrants continued coming in from the East and purchased land along the river.

1824   The new government of Mexico re-defined territories as States, but joined the two separate territories of Texas and Mexico into one State. The capital was moved to Saltillo and orders for the transfer of the archives, the documents that contained the only record of land grants, were issued. Texans were to be allowed one representative in the State government and Coahuila was allowed twelve.

Under the leadership of Jose Antonio Saucedo, the political chief at San Antonio, a number of armed citizens gathered in Alamo Plaza in protest.

1826   In opposition to Mexican rule the Fredonian Rebellion broke out at Nacogdoches. The revolution lasted only one month and sixteen days but it contributed greatly to changes in immigration laws.

1829   Jose Manuel Mier y Teran, who had served as the head of a commission to establish the boundary between the U.S. and Mexico, and had served on the committee on colonization, planned a military expedition "to cut short those intrigues by which the department (of Texas) is undeniably agitated." Mier y Teran was the author of the Law of 1830 except for the article which prohibited further immigration from the U.S.

1830   Law of April 30 prohibiting further immigration was passed.

1832   Battle of Anahuac.

Battle of Velasco.

1834   Santa Anna seized dictatorial power in Mexico heightening discontent not only in Texas but in other parts of Mexico and Yucatan.

1835   General Cos defeated by Texans in the Siege of Bexar. Milam was killed in battle. Cos was routed from the Alamo and forced to surrender on December 10th.

Bexar, as San Antonio was now called, became "the key to the situation in Texas."

1836   February 23rd. The lookout in the tower of San Fernando Church sighted the approach of the army of Santa Anna and rang the alarm. The small Texan force retreated into the Alamo.

February 24th. The Siege of the Alamo began.

March 6th. The Alamo fell.